A Distant Englishness

John Whitehouse

Clayhanger Press

Newcastle-under-Lyme & Douglas, Isle of Man

This book or any portion thereof may not be reproduced or used in any manner whatsoever without the express written permission of the copyright holder except for the use of brief quotations in a book review.

The right of John Whitehouse to be identified as the author of this work has been asserted by him in accordance with the Copyright, Design and Patents Act 1988.

Typeset in Times Roman and Goudy Old Style

First Printing, 2024

Published by Clayhanger Press
82 Eary Veg
Douglas
Isle of Man
IM2 5LZ

www.clayhangerpress.co.uk

All rights reserved.

ISBN-13: 978-1-917017-02-2

Acknowledgements

The following poems have been published previously:

Midnight Cranes, *Orbis,* Issue 192 (2020)
Daisy's dock, *Acumen,* Issue 102 (2022)
The fall, *Acumen,* Issue 106 (2023)
He done me wrong, *Prole,* Issue 34 (2023)

Cover image:

Paper Cuts and Coal
Ink on paper with rubber stamps and paper cuts, 38.87 x 38.51 cm. Abi Whitehouse Instagram.com/_little_abiwhitehouse

A Distant Englishness

Dedication

To my wife Pen, and my five children.

Contents

Foreword by Tamar Yoseloff	8
Introduction	9
In the Boat House	12
Daisy's dock	13
Creosote	14
Midnight Cranes	15
Ball Bearings	16
The fall	17
Starving millions	18
Dogmas	19
Dead Bait	20
Radical geometry	21
Jerome's field	22
A distant Englishness	23
A quiet uncoupling	25
The name of the world	26
An uncommon language	27
Lay down	28
A Psalm for a Pithead	29
The racketeers	30
A complicated kindness	31
Divided Self	32
He done me wrong	33
Misplaced wives	34
The knife thrower	35
Halloween Fair	36
Collecting Du Maurier	37
Burnt	38
The salt villages	39
Skeleton in a tree	40
Meditation	41

Foreword

John Whitehouse's poems journey to places no longer on the map. He speaks of the pits (quoting DH Lawrence) as 'accidents on the landscape', but those 'accidents' have been covered over, so that the traces of earlier industry are barely visible. Whitehouse's goal is to recover these lost sites, that goal made more difficult by his aphasia, the result of a stroke some years ago. But I would say as challenging as he finds the struggle to create words, the resulting poems succeed in excavating the locations of his childhood, where coal dust floats in the air, along with the smell of creosote and lye, Du Maurier cigarettes and sour grass. Whitehouse's pit country is both precise and surreal, a place that existed, but now remains only in dream. Ultimately it is 'the faulty rubbings of men', to use one of Whitehouse's phrases that is the subject of the book – how we construct worlds of work and leisure, toppling them when one system is replaced by another which is more economically viable. This book honours the lives of the miners (the poet's father included) and finds dignity and beauty in the Cannock Chase of the past, a distant Englishness Whitehouse returns to in these poems.

Tamar Yoseloff

Introduction

I remember Norton Canes, the Norman church, the Domesday Book. The old village, with its pretty houses, the books stacked on window shelves, the long magic lawns, Views to the Wrekin.

Around the church, no one dug for coal. It was untouched by the industrial revolution. Paradoxically, a half a mile up the road, it was gold rush country. Millions of tons of coal a week were mined in Cannock Chase coalfields. The trains crisscrossed the landscape, like a cloud front. Holding up the traffic, spreading a sulphurous stink, grit in your eye, ash in your hair, slattering close to the houses.

To borrow a phrase from DH Lawrence, the pits 'were accidents on the landscape.' Three hundred feet of slag rising upwards, its peak an unfinished sculpture, still smouldering. The cooler part became a six-million-ton mountain range, with trees and bindweed, and strange water lilied pools, in the foothills around which dragonflies hummed in the summer.

Coal rubs out our natural history, spills a tilth of scrap iron, tin clippings, making a new heavy-metal soil. The canals turned green, wharves sprouting sour grass, a yellow cascade of dandelions grow in the cuttings. I grew up with this difference, two kinds of Englishness in plain sight of one another.

I didn't notice the havoc of where I lived. I had built a childhood around a constantly changing world, sliding under both perceptions – a world fringed by soughing trees and lavender meadows, red diesel smells left by the tractor, and the desolation of the pits.

In time, the trains were decommissioned, and the canal barges left to rot in their basins. The slag heaps, so mighty they could block the light of the sun, went down, sliced like a piece of cheese in a grater.

Speculative builders sewed up the gaping holes of coal mines, the wheelhouse, the slums of the miners, held up with rings of iron. They replaced them with a spurious newness. Private homes, cul-de-sacs. But the lie of the land remained, like markers to another life.

The new occupants puzzle over railway sleepers buried oddly in their gardens. They dig down for temples, or Roman remains, but find guiltless fields, where the venture capitalists lost their moral compass.

Having aphasia, I am in good company. Baudelaire, Emerson, Beckett and many others. But I am not the man I was before the stroke, where I flicked the magic whip of semantics, choosing ever-more beguiling phrases, conversations that go on forever.

My voice is like a faulty microphone, I can't remember the alphabet, or read aloud. My comprehension is weak, a blotter cloaks my brain. Others talk at 135 words a minute, telling jokes that I do not follow. But I have hope.

Samuel Beckett, in a conversation with the author Lawrence Shainberg, said of aphasia: 'With diminished concentration, loss of memory, obscured intelligence – what you, for example, might call 'brain damage' – the more chance there is for saying something closest to what one really is.' That's what I really want to do, but prior to that, there are many things to unlearn.

John Whitehouse, May 2024

The Poems

In the Boat House

My eyes adjust, temperature drops, empty
boats dip. I gaze at the mirrored water
tangled in the canvas awning of the roof,

laughing and shifting. I sit in the burden
of the boat, gripping the gunwale as we
pull out, oars sweeping stroke after stroke,

my father's strong back, cotton motes
falling from his white shirt, coal dust floating
in the air, as he reaches out for something.

Daisy's dock

I can hear my feet nightwalking on the tracks,
overhead a light is hanging yellow and black,
yellow and black, rehearsing

the downfall of the railway bridge, signalling the
end of something, like the light at the end of
Daisy's dock, in Scott Fitzgerald's novel.

A Ford Anglia is dangling from the railway bridge,
misled by a green light. Indicators flashing, blanching
against the beige paintwork.

The independent suspension is showing coquettishly,
like the ankles of country girls. Coal black rain flooding
the underpass, two fathoms deep,

ready for a stealthy drowning. Or to give us passage
to the other side. Reaching the water's edge, a canoe
is chafing, lapping at my feet.

Creosote

A damselfly is rising,
uplifted by a waft of hot
creosote, tilting the air
smothering a fragrance.

The reek of the old
wooden school, bleached
telegraph poles, sedation
of railway sleepers.

A wharf with sour grass,
sunken canal barges.
Old men gazing up
through the waters.

Midnight Cranes

Older folk choose lesser gods to
deliver them. They raise their eyes
to construction site cranes tainting
their lounges yellow.

An engine starts, car doors slam,
tyres slither, skittering to get away
from the double-glazed flat, in search
of somewhere normal.

Above, my father watches a parched
shape vanishing in the snow.
In his agony, an electric star sustains him.
Beyond it, a heart-breaking sky.

Ball bearings

Words fall from her mouth
on a glass-topped table.
She holds one up to the light,

its steely brightness visible.
He hears it, slung into a threat,
starts scoring the adamant rock,

a crack to be prised open,
panicking at goodbye, recasting
love into nodding acquaintance.

In the dark, he feared a piece
of the city had come adrift,
crashing into his house.

The fall

happened overnight. Cloaking houses, chimney pots,
altering architecture,

the air we breathe, palpable, a white-out of corrections.
Crumping underfoot

the postman's steps as he slides past obliterated shops,
blitzed gables,

a drift of useless cars. Somewhere a muffled phone rings
buried underground.

Starving millions

Gaunt students on the top floor
track-suit tops zipped against the weather,
hiding shaven heads like question-

marks among the black and white,
daring to run from the affront of poetry.
They smile at their banal messages,

sing brave songs on the window ledge,
write in felt-tip on the brutalist columns:
England's Starving Millions.

They stuff *The Sun* into their kit bags,
phones ringing like plumbers on a break
missing their white vans.

Make a run for it now, across the car park!
White vertical stripes of their track suits
disappearing in the snow.

The bright colours of their graffiti
count for nothing. Their lives are blighted,
like malachite on brass.

Dogmas

She had a critical eye, scrubbing floorboards
with softwood lye. Watching it dry slowly.
A crafty communion of mark-making.

Her daubs had no place in the old dogmas.
A Muslim clean shaven, a Christian drunk,
nothing representable, nothing certain.

Oil paint gets into the stir-fry. A rancid odour
steeps her clothes. Pools of demonic colours
spattering her shoes with red-hot pokers,

an improvised jazz tempo, spilling jeopardy,
coming from a crack under the floor. Dangerous
liaisons, living arrhythmically.

Paintings hang on our conflicted walls. A ritual
to remove turpentine, quelling hands with cream.
Her fists sprout anarchic fingers.

Dead bait

She dipped her fingers into a bowl of plain water making marks on whitewashed walls, languidly imagining a man's face. She watches the droplets evaporate on her fingers, hears voices outside.

His face crowds the walls of her studio. A fragrance of sandalwood, the smell of his shirts, strong hands with square-cut nails. The painted man isn't her lover, she draws him for other lives.

A man casts a lure into the lake, a reel singing out, counting blue as it lands in the rise of the swell, swinging its hips like a samba. Pikes grin, silhouettes moving in for the kill, trained assassins.

Radical geometry

Carpenters make the best slaughterers. A rough
correctness, a sureness of touch

sizing up how you're standing, making shapes
in their heads, the knife ready,

dreaming of you on their work bench, auguring
the cut with their paring chisels.

In medieval times, adzes smoothed the way to
cathedrals or the great 14th-century barns,

standing in the way of a third Heathrow runway.
They could mortise and tenon you now

using radical geometry for an alphabet, making you
into freshly-made kebabs.

But they retreat into history, longbows nocked,
sheaves of arrows falling.

Jerome's field

Children play on consecrated ground, peeking
tremulously at the Jerome Clapp Colliery,
their ever-blackened neighbour.

The owner preached hellfire in a hot tin chapel
ringed by brimstone, shovelling coal
into the mouths of his flock.

Slag heaps rise, accidents on the landscape.
Unwanted children left to splutter
in the heat, left to play on the dark side

of the moon. A six-million-ton mountain,
sprawling like a naked girl, brazen
centrefold for the Chalk Man.

Tractors veer around them, knitting a green slash,
sowing seed potatoes like landmines,
exploding into sapphire dragonflies

on the zephyr wind, flitting between worlds.
We are so unlike angels, adoring gimcrack,
the faulty rubbings of men.

A distant Englishness

The day was misshapen
a clock in a painting
melting like camembert
in the haze.

Father was Omo white,
smelling of childhood,
Reckitt's Blue in the
round stone bowl.

He sent me for a pint.
I cycled triumphant,
a victory wave to grottoes
framed by cast iron,

to the green baize swards
of Eden. I forgot the ashpit,
Daddies Sauce, salt cellars,
a naked bookshelf.

Here are white porticoes,
lawns sewn with magic
seeds, long fragrances,
books stacked in halls.

I stroked a DS Citroen,
heat slowed my breath.
A goddess in blue delphinium,
her empty steering wheel,

englobing the church,
swathed in Saint George's flag,
Pat Boone sings from the manse:
Love Letters in the Sand.

I met the landlord's glittering eye,
bathed him with Gilead's balm
in the off-licence. He didn't
give me change.

An old van slouched towards me,
windows open. On the dash,
three mean dials. In the back,
a woman hitching her bra,

garnering immense flesh.
Shiny Martian shale, zipping
underneath me. Bottles fizzing,
rattling on the handlebars.

A quiet uncoupling

At the crest of the hill, it began snowing. Blurring
what was real, swirling the violated soil, a tilth
of radioactive tin clippings.

Seen at a distance, my home was pretty
in the Black Country blizzard. Buried by a crackling
rime of Pneumococci.

Outside my friends new house, I saw a firebird
of a car, Vauxhall Cresta, chariot red and ivory,
tyres painted white.

Train sets have a sparky odour, ozone and gun-
smoke uncoupling our worlds. I came down
quickly, on a ski lift,

past smothered houses, obliterated sheds,
smelling the stubborn sweat on my anorak.
Tyres making a perfect line in the snow.

The Name of the World

An imperfect Mappa Mundi, Jerusalem at its centre,
spreads out, carrying the misshapen world: a road sign
misspelt. Spent lingua franca, worthless insignias,
poetry for the dog-eared.

Beyond the map of love, our pockets are nearly empty –
a battered lighter, a photograph of a girl, a perfume bottle.
Fuck is an exclamation mark, a siren blaring
in the afternoon heat,

as if we have unearthed oaths buried in a forest, a bride
chosen in the windbreak of language. Or found them
floating as red balloons, over the frank arses of dogs
shitting in the leaves.

I use a hammer to smash the glass of language, leading
dried-up letters to water, shouting their names. A psalm
to the blue ocean, the half-hung moon. Worn-out copper
for burnished gold.

An uncommon language

I taste fealty in the buttery tang of windfalls.
A sharp zip of loyalty in a Black Country Dick –
golden pears plucked in a free-for-all garden,
infusing Perry wine into John Bull Englishness.

A reek of creosoted sleepers, a knot of steel
looped around us. Ley lines under the maisonettes,
clocking on at Carpets-4-U. Offices with sleek
colourways, unfurnished rooms, aloof new estates.

She landed awkwardly, a moth born for migration,
Hunter's dashed in the mud, an expensive camel coat,
drawing sidelong glances from the crowd. Caught
betraying their last supper with a camera flash.

They read her article, mouths full of Parkin cake.
Black Country Dick Rises Again. Their vision carries
to the edge of the village. Mercury lights daub
red cars with a treacherous sheen of yellow.

Lay down

My father wore a gangster's hat,
a coal blue cicatrix circled his brow,
an unseen note from the underground,
a shadowy map,

fingers lighting dynamite's fuse,
hands steady as a carpenter, white
with fear, dreaming of wheat gathered
from these ashen fields.

His frame rattled the plate-glass
windows of Woolworths. He skirted
traffic, racing to the bus stop, tumbling,
arse over tit at my feet,

a bag of broken biscuits strewn
in the road, a red ball whirling like a skull,
a guttering candle. His blood drains
through the gravel.

We went upstairs, his arm jovial
behind me. We ate the blood-stained biscuits.
He tells stories of fires, rockfalls
and near misses.

From the bus, I see new houses
up for sale. Sleek colourways, rolling
garage doors, their angular lawns
pointing into one another.

The pit is decked with flowers,
I think of him, part of the mutated earth.
The magic of his hands, like Aaron's rod,
bearing ripe fruit and almonds.

A Psalm for a Pithead

Shut the winding gear, empty the locks
let barges rot in their folk-art colours.
Free the pit ponies from their stocks
let them canter on the yellow strand.

Unravel the railways, decouple the trucks
turn slagheaps into cheese, rind sliced
with a wire. Liquefy the iron trains.
The scales have fallen from your eyes.

Spool back the tape, past mourning wives
crying at the pithead, to a gladdening river
beckoning you bathe in raiment's white,
laving your body in the healing spray.

The racketeers

After swindling the riff-raff, the slick
racketeers built houses in three colours:
magical, maniacal, nonsensical,

a river in spate, carrying a flood of double-
glazing, light glinting off a tilt-and-turn
window, caught in the decanting,

sewing villages together, with Astro turf.
Mowers against the grain, vertical stripes
correcting the larkspur, bluebells,

burying all the mobsters sins under a brick
cenotaph. To remember the war-dead of
another country, silent in the ground.

A complicated kindness

We have cultivated earthly things –
certifying that there nothing for us
on the other side –

sunburnt pensioners in deckchairs
looking out to sea, sharing
a complicated kindness.

Would it matter if we parted company
under a Red Sea moon, never seeing
one another again,

awaiting our fate as stardust or decay?
Our fathers fastened a knot around us,
a dissenter's religion,

fluked to the ocean's floor. We danced
against the barbs, drifting to land,
sketching what we saw.

If there is a future, I would write it down on
unsullied scrolls. Choosing what you want,
or never dreamt of,

I see you in a softening light, unwrapping
untroubled dreams. Ready to set on fire
dells of paradise.

The divided self

This garden party reminds me
of the differences in our childhoods;
a rip of the main artery, a rupture –
between you and me.

Twilight houses, white colonnades,
night scents, soft lawns stretching
to the road, fringed by a walled garden,
divide us even further.

Murmurs of a good time, flashy talk,
lea grass fleeing to the woods.
An overpowering smell of magnolias
undercut by a stench of gold.

Children play volleyball, their fathers
join in, switching to night manoeuvres,
bawling like wild animals. They pummel
the air, making a hole in nature.

On the towpath, music mumbles far off
a T.V. commercial selling desire. The canal
is a ruined church, red and blue barges
sinking into a leprous marsh.

He done me wrong

but I'd like to dress him for the funeral.
A silk blue coat, a grey knitted tie,
Italian shirt, Hermes cufflinks,
Dior aftershave, worn for the pretty girls.

He done me wrong, I caught them at it,
frozen in comic nudity, the last hurrah.
But I'd like to dress him for the funeral,
after the men have finished laying him out,

lamp light falling softly on the vase
holding the lilies. I will fetch warm water,
kneel to wash his body, tousle his hair, say
a private hallelujah, and let him be buried.

Misplaced wives

A silent shape crosses the bedroom. She dresses for alterity –
filmic romantic, and unreachable.

Shall I iron my existence flat, like a shirt hanging off a wire,
smoothed into shape, begging for absolution?

I stand by the window in the children's room. Humpty Dumpty
wallpaper, Lego showered on the floor.

A duplicitous yellow car brakes to a stop. A man jumps out,
pisses like a racehorse, waving nonchalantly.

An amateur film, blurred with scratchy memories,
as if it had been found in a loft somewhere.

The knife thrower

As he sat eating, the knife thrower said he had no conversation. He was raised by gypsies.

Did you ever miss? He shrugged, looked down to breadcrumbs, freshly slaughtered salad.

She undid her blouse. The marks from a bowie knife in her shoulder, worn and resolute.

Halloween

Cries in the inkberry night show bewitchery. Music
on loudspeakers, hammering a hundred bullets into me,
jittery and rapturous,

luminous bulbs, tongues of Holy Spirit. Ferris wheels
whirling into space, seeing the mirrored arc of the world,
candy floss floats upwards.

The chapels have been tranquilised, devil-free, like Bethlehem.
Shiftless jack-o'-lanterns, riding the waltzers, spinning the girls
eternally, in a Danse Macabre.

Collecting Du Maurier

My ready-made art was spinning from cars, down
to summer grass. *Lucky Strike* for the trucks, *Stuyvesant*
for the skiers, *Park Drive* for the Anglia drivers,

Du Maurier for the Jaguars, with their leather interiors,
gliding to London. Red and gold flip tops
open onto walnut, like a gilt case.

In the traffic roar, I reached up for honey
hanging from the hedgerows. *Pasha, Ardath, Camel,
Passing Clouds, Sweet Afton Banks.*

Burnt

Mr Greco arrives on a Vespa,
zooming across the playground
one leg out, like a TT rider.

Fumbling in his pockets
he finds a pack of Lucky Strikes.
Strips the warm cellophane,

takes a cigarette, sets his face
aflame with a silver lighter, shiny
as a flick-knife.

He exhales a plume of smoke.
Skims the burning stub to the earth,
a stricken warplane.

The rest, spread in his palm, he throws
aloft, a soft wind winnowing
the sweet tobacco.

Teaching you will be just like that!
Our frail bodies fragmenting, falling to
the waste-paper basket.

The salt villages

On the first day the counter tops in the art room
brimmed with salt villages.

We were left quite alone, trying to figure out
what the Arctic igloos meant.

We picked them up, lighter than air, zooming
like model aeroplanes.

With his suit of lights, the art teacher grabbed the cloth,
jerked it upwards,

flew it like a flag. Salt igloos, hailstones as big
as bowling balls, swirled in the storm.

We've seen the trick many times on *Sunday Night
at the Palladium:* Cups and saucers unmoved,

unbroken. Above the igloos, Northern Lights failed –
we became fretful of the Arctic night.

Skeleton in a tree

Driving on a winter's night, leaves gone from the oaks,
I caught a glimpse of a fox's skeleton,

hard cheese yellow. Gibbeted up, in the tree. Crucified,
for our sins, a traitor in a metal cage.

Like the young man, found dead in a railway tunnel without
a mark or a rope. Just the shudder of the sea,

tired of all humanity, lonely at its edges. Listen to its roar,
a call beyond forest and field.

Meditation

I have witnessed
an old man sat on
a rank bed, 4 a.m.
hands clasped.

Is he praying,
or saying a psalter,
to an unmendable
crack in his life?

He rises, looks at
his stoic hands.
Thinks of grief,
how that will be.

The Author

John Whitehouse is a retired academic who lives in London. He suffers from aphasia, which affects him with immediate comprehension, word selection and memory. Post stroke, his work has been in: *Interpreters' House, Acumen, Frogmore Papers, Snakeskin, Other Poetry, French Literary Review,* and *Cannons Mouth*. He won the Commended Prize in the 2021 *Creative Future* competition and received an Arts Council Grant.

Cover Design by Clayhanger Press
Front Cover image Abi Whitehouse

Typesetting & Design Roger Bloor
Copy Editor Sara Levy

www.clayhangerpress.co.uk

Printed in Great Britain
by Amazon